BASICS - A BEGINNER'S GUIDE TO STAGE MANAGEMENT

Peter Coleman

ENTERTAINMENT
TECHNOLOGY PRESS

Educational Series

BASICS – A BEGINNER'S GUIDE TO STAGE MANAGEMENT

Peter Coleman

Entertainment Technology Press

Basics – A Beginner's Guide to Stage Management

© Peter Coleman

First edition Published June 2007 by
Entertainment Technology Press Ltd
The Studio, High Green, Great Shelford, Cambridge CB22 5EG
Internet: www.etnow.com

ISBN 978 1 904031 47 5

A title within the
Entertainment Technology Press Educational Series
Series editor: John Offord

CODE / BSM

CONTENTS

A GOOD DSM IS LIKE GOLD 9

INTRODUCTION 11

1   SO WHAT IS STAGE MANAGEMENT? 13

2   WHY IS IT IMPORTANT? 19

3   CUEING OR 'CALLING' THE SHOW, THE PROMPT BOOK ..25

4   THE HARDWARE 33

5   TRAINING FOR STAGE MANAGEMENT 41

6   CONCLUSIONS 43

THE STAGE MANAGEMENT ASSOCIATION 45

FURTHER READING 47

GLOSSARY 49

ACKNOWLEDGEMENTS

With thanks to: Antonia Collins and Barbara Eifler of the Stage Masnagement Association, to Alan Ayckbourn for permission to print an extract from his book *The Crafty Art of Playmaking*, and to John Offord and Jackie Staines at Entertainment Technology Press for their usual assistance.

A GOOD DSM IS LIKE GOLD

The DSM (Deputy Stage Manager), especially in smaller-scale repertory theatres like the Stephen Joseph Theatre, will be the only other person continuously in the room with you from the start to finish of the rehearsal-room period. He or – more often it seems these days – she will notate, report, prompt and generally run the rehearsals on a technical level, ensuring that things proceed smoothly. Other colleagues, namely the Stage Manager and ASM (assistant stage manager), will be less in evidence, involved as they are in the assembling of props, small items of furniture and occasionally even in the construction of various items.

The working relationship you have with your DSM is important. Few will wish to intrude on the artistic side, unless asked, but they can help to point out the occasional inconsistency which you and the actors have overlooked: 'He handed his umbrella to the porter in scene three. How can he still have it?' Their role ranges from this sort of thing, right through to a smile of encouragement when a scene suddenly takes off for the first time. We all need a bit of that.

The DSM is also very useful when it comes to gently reminding an actor for the fifth time that they have their main speech in Act One entirely back to front. It's an unpopular job, but someone has to do it.

The DSM is often the production's lifeline to the outside world and keeps the rest of the team informed as to production changes and updates. A rehearsal report is issued each day. 'The dining table will need to be strong enough to stand on,' 'Miss Wilkins needs Wellington boots for the start of scene three.'

Work on maintaining a good relationship between you and the DSM; share every detail. Once you get into the theatre, especially during the fraught period known as the technical rehearsal ('the tech'), the well-briefed DSM, fully appraised of your intentions, can save your life.

Alan Ayckbourn in *The Crafty Art of Playmaking*
published by Faber and Faber, 2002
reproduced by permission of the author

INTRODUCTION

Those familiar with all of the other *Basics* publications, may be a little surprised that stage management is going to get the *Basic* treatment, after all it's hardly a subject that will contain lots of information about the technical equipment found in the performance space. Well, there are odd bits here and there, but not much. No, this is a topic all about systems and people, without which most of that technical equipment used by others in the performance workplace couldn't function, well at least not function properly.

For those who have not worked in professional, or indeed, most amateur theatre, the first thing to take on board is that the term stage management actually refers to a team of people and it's this team, and their actions relating to the other technical disciplines, that makes the whole performance event work. For some of you just starting out in the theatre world, you may not yet quite realise just how important the stage management function can be. It's a fair assumption that 99% of the population (even non-theatrical people) have heard the expression "stage managed". Well, I hope that these next few pages will make the title a little more meaningful and help you understand exactly what *real* stage management is all about.

There are just three main aspects that this book is going to attempt to cover concerning stage management, the first being why you need stage management in the first place. The second aspect is just what it is that stage management actually does. And in describing the second element you will start to see the answers to the first. Thirdly, there is the "how to do it" part - or at least some of the important factors involved.

Over the years I have seen countless instances, almost exclusively within education based events and some amateur users, where the stage management function has not only been ignored, but totally omitted from the operation of mounting a stage production. It's rather sad that at an educational level this vital facet of the performance technical team has not been given the critical importance it deserves. It seems that it's not until you move on to higher levels of education, within the drama school environment, that you actually come across the stage management function working in the right way. With the help of this book I hope you will consider putting this situation right.

For those of you entering into some type of formal stage management training, maybe within a drama school, please remember that this is *Basics* and as such may not give every detail of the stage management job, but certainly from the technical equipment and organisational viewpoint it should give you some useful information and some pointers about what's in store for you.

In all the other *Basics* publications I can claim to have had quite a lot of practical hands-on experience with the technical matters discussed, because over the years in various places I have done the jobs, solved the problems, even stayed with the technical discipline long enough to get the proverbial tee shirt, but a basics book on stage management? No, I've never been a stage manager so why am I attempting to describe the functions of it here? Simply because in a theatrical performance, it's important. No, it's vital! Having worked in all of the other technical disciplines I've had to work alongside the stage management team, so I feel quite well placed to describe some of the details of what they do.

This wouldn't be a *Basics* publication without an alternative title or two, so just to prepare you for what's to come, how about: "Is that what they do all day?" or "I always wondered who did that".

1 SO WHAT IS STAGE MANAGEMENT?

So just what is stage management? Well, when you look closely at all of the tasks that fall into the stage management portfolio you might start to wonder if the job title is correct.

It's a rather strange job and a little like the acting company or other technical people involved in the performance, the job is split into two parts. There's the 'day job' or at least those things which need to happen during the normal working hours of a day: 9 to 5. Then there's the performance, when all the preparation, planning and expertise are put to use. This not only makes for some very long days, but there is a distinct split and a big difference in what each half of the job entails.

I will make some distinctions between the world of professional stage management and the amateur and educational use of the title. This has got nothing to do with the status that some may perceive exists between the two – I have seen some very good amateur stage managers. It's more to do with the practical issues involved. In order to understand this you will need to understand a little of what takes place in each sector.

Within the professional theatre workplace, the stage management team will generally be responsible for the actions and the wellbeing of the acting company. They will be well versed if not 100% skill proficient in many of the technical disciplines involved in performance works, i.e. they may not be able to operate the lighting or sound control as would a dedicated technician, or mend a costume or build a piece of scenery, but they will understand the requirements involved. I used the term 'team' because in the professional workplace the tasks that they undertake require stage management in numbers, not just one figurehead stage manager.

It's worthy of note that going back in time a mere 50 years or so, professional theatres all had someone with the title of stage manager whose responsibility it was to organise all of the technical side of performance events on stage, but with very little contact or control over the acting company. During this time the acting company would also have a stage manager and team of stage management personnel, sometimes known as the 'company stage manager' in order to differentiate the roles of responsibility. As time has passed, within a venue the technical side of the theatre job has changed, the title of stage manager has become more correctly re-named as 'technical manager' or 'technical director' leaving the 'stage manager' title for use by those looking after the acting company.

So back to more modern times, the team of stage management at a professional level will normally be not less than three people: the stage manager, deputy stage manager (DSM) and assistant stage manager (ASM), obviously in order of seniority. In a large company this may extend to five, six, or more people. The deputy and the assistant numbers will be increased to meet the demands of the department.

The starting place, the first rung of the ladder of stage management, is the ASM, often regarded as the lowest and most menial member of the team. On day one an ability to make the tea is just about all that's expected, and there are plenty of people around who will tell them that they don't even know how to do that! But they rapidly learn the skills and tasks associated with stage management. After a little experience the ASM graduates to the position of DSM, being given a little more responsibility which will usually include the actual running or 'calling' of the show. There will be lots more about this particular function as we progress. Then finally, probably after several years more experience, there is the position of stage manager, where the job will often include the organising and scheduling of the whole stage management department.

In dealing with the needs and requirements of the acting company, the stage management function will vary widely depending upon what has become the norm in any particular company structure, where their works will include what you might regard as a high level of pastoral care. This facet of stage management life is very dependent upon the style of the performance company. Where it is resident in a venue, this element may be minimal but where it's moving between venues (on tour) there may be quite a lot of 'nursemaiding' to be done, in sorting out travel and accommodation requirements and just keeping tracks on the acting company to ensure that they all arrive in the right place at the right time. I used the term 'pastoral' meaning to point towards someone in charge of a flock, in this case a flock of actors. I wonder what you call a group of actors? Surely not just the acting company? No we won't go there. But it's quite often the case that the stage manager is seen as something between a mother or father confessor, a doctor, babysitter, tax inspector, safety deposit box and taxi driver all rolled into one and that all before they actually attempt to do the stage management job proper.

There are so many facets of what the stage management team has to do. Take, for example, a stage production that involves food and drink being a part of the action. After some careful and often detailed detective work in finding out who amongst the acting company will or won't eat a particular food, someone has to go and do the shopping, probably on a daily basis, and then it's all got to be prepared and of course set out for the acting company, not forgetting the clearing up afterwards.

Then there's the matter of personal props – these could be anything from a lighter and a packet of cigarettes, to a walking stick or a pair of spectacles. Someone has to find the article in question and, having been the referee between the director and the performer who might have rather different views about what is suitable, make sure that the things are actually in possession of the performer before they go on stage. A time-served and resourceful stage manager will have taken the precaution of assembling a selection of stand-by or 'reserve' items where personal props are concerned. In the unlikely event that a performer 'mislays' that critical personal prop, then such a reserve can be a real life saver.

The task of finding things, quite often including set dressings and furniture which you might have thought are the responsibility of the set designer, can take up hours of time and organisation. More of this later. When all of the mundane daily grind of finding, fetching and carrying, preparation and checking has taken place, there is still the small matter of keeping track of the acting company personnel. This tends to be a continual ongoing process, monitored practically 24 hours a day, because if a cast member is ill or incapacitated in any way, then the stage management need to know about it as soon as possible in case an understudy should be required with all the additional work that that will entail.

At this point I have left out the other major factor in the life of stage management – the rehearsals in the run-up to the production – left out, but not forgotten, and I shall return to this a little later.

So at the business end of the day we get to that other different element of work that I mentioned earlier, the performance. I think most people are probably familiar with the timescales and timings involved here, but being Basics it's worth going over it in some detail. The stage management, or at least one member of the team, will usually be at the venue 1½ hours before curtain up and everyone – stage management and the acting company, will be there by 'the half' – that's 35 minutes before the scheduled start time.

In theatre terms, assuming a start time of 7.30pm:

The ½ hour is called at 6.55pm

The ¼ hour is called at 7.10pm

The 5 minute call is made at 7.20pm

And "Act 1 or Overture and Beginners" is made at 7.25pm.

Stage management, specifically the person calling or cueing the show (more of this a little later) will be in contact with the FOH (Front of House) staff who will give clearance for the performance to begin. This can sometimes be a rather fraught process, which will vary across the performance styles and venues for any number of good reasons. It may be that a couple of coach parties have been delayed and that it's better to delay the start for five minutes, rather than have fifty or a hundred people trying to find their seats in the dark and ruining the concentration of the rest of the audience who are trying to concentrate on a wordy dramatic piece of theatre.

Of course, if it were a different style of production this may not be so relevant and some places will work very hard to ensure that the audience is all seated by the appointed time, even not permitting entry by latecomers until a suitable break in the performance.

So the stage management will receive clearance from FOH. They are then responsible for starting the performance and what some might describe as the 'real' work of the stage management team takes place – those actions and functions which are involved in the running of the technical things that make the performance happen. That could be the ASM making a live sound effect off stage or giving and receiving small items of property to the acting company as they enter and exit the stage. Then there are the actions of the DSM or stage manager in making calls to the acting company to ensure that they are on stage in time to make their entrance and last, but by no means least, the technical cueing or 'calling' of the show.

There may be one other function that falls to the remit of the stage management, or more specifically that member of the team who is cueing or calling the show, that is the 'prompt'. Now in some productions and venues there may be a rule or an agreement by the acting company, usually led by the director of the piece, that if a member of the acting company 'dries' then they are on their own and they have to get out of the situation as best they can, while in other more traditional productions a prompt may be given, maybe just a word or two or maybe half a line, just to get the flow of words going again. In general in the professional theatre world the use of the dedicated prompter has more or less died out*, leaving this function to the member of stage management who is cueing or calling the show, for that person will have the script or libretto in the case of a musical event, open and in front of them. This is often referred to as the 'prompt book' or 'prompt script' which they have annotated with all of the technical requirements and cues needed within the piece, and since it contains all the text, they will be expected to provide the prompt.

It's at this point that I would highlight the main difference between the professional and the amateur forms of stage management. To be strictly fair it's not necessarily due to a failing of the stage management functions, more likely that they are simply not tasked to undertake the one critical function that's needed in all performance activities, that of cueing or calling the show. Sadly, a good number of amateurs and education events simply don't cue or call their shows at all. They leave the whole issue of cueing to the technical discipline involved, so that the lighting and the sound operators are forced to take their own cues, either by reading the text from a script or libretto, or by reading notes containing specific lines of text or notable actions within the production, or even by trying to remember the actions and timing involved.

For me this just won't do, because those technical operators just won't have time to be reading text or notes while concentrating on the operation of the equipment they are tasked to operate.

In lots of amateur productions, the other function which is handled differently is that of the prompt, for where I have said that in most professional productions the dedicated prompter is a thing of the past, in some amateur productions things have more or less remained as the norm. If you think about it, everyone, amateur or professional, will be able to learn and remember their lines, but for the professional who may know the piece in performance from a previous rendition and be performing it for many days, weeks or even months, their likelihood of forgetting their lines is far less than an amateur performer, who may have less rehearsal time and only perform the piece on a few occasions, so they might need a little more help in the prompting department.

So to recap and clarify: the stage management team won't be building the set or scenery, they won't be rigging, focusing and operating the lighting, they don't make up pre-recorded sound effects or operate the sound system in

---

* The exception is probably the 'repetitéur', a person usually only found in large grand opera productions who speaks or prompts the singers with words or lines of dialogue, often to aid the pronunciation of the foreign language involved.

performance, they don't set the scenery on stage or operate the flying system (assuming the space has one), they don't make the costumes, paint the sets, dress the acting company, do the laundry, take the tickets from the audience or sell the ice cream in the interval. Have I left anything out? You can probably see where this is leading because, apart for all the things they don't do, they probably do everything else. Yes, before anyone has the urge to tell me I'm wrong, please remember I did say early on that the stage management team needed to have a basic level of understanding of everything involved in performance works, but under normal conditions, whatever 'normal' is in theatre terms, they will be too busy concentrating on the stage management functions to be involved with all those other things.

The stage manager coordinates the technical rehearsal.

2 WHY IS IT IMPORTANT?

Well I've probably provided most of the answers to that question during chapter 1, but to clarify and expand the reasons involved, let me start by simply saying that stage management provide the links that join a whole production together. These links aid and affect every person and discipline involved in the performance, and some you might find rather odd, or even expect to find other people and dedicated departments looking after them. By way of further explanation let's make up a fictitious 'job description' for the position of a stage manager:

The successful applicant will be expected to show practical experience and ability in the following areas:

- To schedule and organise the daily running of the department (team of three)
- To liaise with resident and visiting directors in the schedules for rehearsals
- Have a comprehensive portfolio of stage management works and achievements
- Be able to read music (please state if proficient in any specific instrument)
- Show any related speciality, e.g. prop making
- Hold a full driving licence (driving light vans up to three tonnes may be required)
- Be computer literate (formerly have the ability to type)
- First aid qualification would be an advantage
- Equity membership is assumed

In the world of professional stage management, some personnel will be Equity (actors' union) members, and many professional stage managers belong to the Stage Management Association.

The problem is that so much of what stage management actually does is hardly ever written down into a job description; it's covered in the title and within the performing arts industry it's understood and accepted that way. So the only way to understand a little more is to break things down further.

Let's start at the beginning, let's assume that a new company is being brought together for a production of what we'll call a straight play, i.e. words and actions only, no singing or dancing.

On the first day the company will probably all meet for the first time for a 'read through'. The first thing that stage management will do is to make sure that they have all the contact names, addresses and telephone numbers of the acting company. This is an important, indeed vital function, even where the company in question may be a local amateur group where everyone assumes that people's contact address and details are known. I mentioned earlier that the stage management team would be in contact with the performance company almost 24 hours a day, well that's not factual or indeed practical but what is normal is that the acting company and the stage management team have a means of contact.

These days the mobile phone has made this task so much easier, but there may still be a requirement, especially within the professional ranks, that the acting company are required to reside within a certain distance of the performance venue. That might be 25 miles or some other distance taken as the norm for a particular company. Sometimes special dispensations are made, where someone may actually live just outside the designated boundary area and of course everyone has a need to travel for all sorts of reasons, and when the show is up and running. If there is nothing for the acting company to do during the day, then to expect them to remain within a specific distance of the venue may be rather unrealistic, but with the vagaries of public transport, mechanical breakdowns, even the odd attack of sod's law, it's important that people are contactable. So the contact list is the first thing that stage management will be responsible for.

At that first day read through, it may be that one of the acting company is absent and it may be that a member of stage management needs to 'read in'. And, of course, who's going to provide the coffee and biscuits? Rehearsals will rapidly move from the reading to the more formalised rehearsal room or space where the acting company will start to get to know the set, its doorways, windows, furniture, etc – rather difficult weeks ahead of the first night, probably before the set has actually been built.

So it falls to stage management to 'mark out' the set and all of its relevant features usually on a plain floor with coloured marking tape, and if not completely accurate, as close a representation to the real end product as possible. Obviously things like chairs and tables and the occasional important practical item like a telephone, table lamp or some other item that has an important part in the action will be set out by stage management in order to provide some sense of realism to the acting company.

This brings about the next task in store for stage management, the notation involved in the 'blocking' of the action. The blocking is the movement and position of the acting company around the stage. It will be determined by the director and will be noted down by stage management, so that in the early days of rehearsal the acting company can check they are in the right place. As rehearsals progress the movements and positions are learned by the acting company just as they remember their lines, which of course brings yet another stage management function. Having said earlier that productions will adopt a house style which will or will not include prompting, in the rehearsal period you might expect that the acting company is not word perfect, so stage management will be on hand with the odd word where needed.

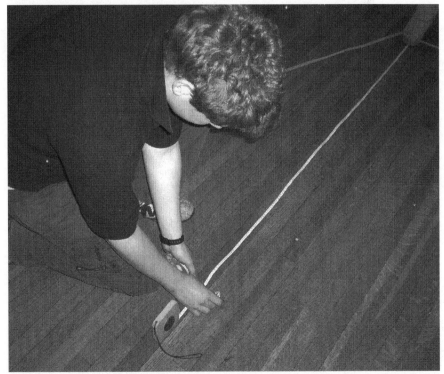

Marking out in the rehearsal room.

While all this is going on within the rehearsal, some of those other tasks that I mentioned previously will be taking place away from the rehearsal room, in the gathering of furniture and set dressings, often simply described as 'properties' a name covering a wide variety of things. If you break down the specifics of what's involved in the average stage set for a straight play, then the actual set and scenery such as doorways, stairs and windows, the actual structure of the set, including its design and painting will normally come under the control of a dedicated department, i.e. scenic carpentry and workshops.

The acting company is just that, and they will wear the costumes provided by the wardrobe department, who might also have an involvement with wigs and hair pieces, although depending upon the nature of the event this may be handled by the individual member of the cast or, in the case of a very large or complicated requirement, have a dedicated wig master in charge of it all. So taking these specifics out of the running, what's left? Well, whatever it is, it's stage management that will be involved with it.

A dictionary entry may offer one variation something like "Property: an article used on stage for a play, etc". So whether it's the carpet or the sofa, the drinks cabinet or the fridge and just about everything else that's not nailed down, and sometimes even when they are, the properties will exercise the stage management team, and they often have rather a thankless task. If the venue they are working in is not blessed with a suitable supply of properties or a specific props department, then the stage management team will be sent out, usually into the local neighbourhood, to persuade, cajole, bribe, even plead with a whole range of people to part with quite often valuable items, "just for a week or two" and of course "we'll take good care of it" and "you'll get a credit in the programme".

So as you can imagine the gathering of properties is never quite straightforward and when they return with the spoils of their pleading and tramping the streets, to be met by the set designer or the director with "oh no that Chinese rug just won't do, it's the wrong shade of green and won't go with the set", you can begin to see why it is such a taxing job. There are certain tasks within the life of stage management that are difficult, and not made any easier when returning those much loved precious and valuable items, when having to explain just why the antique refectory table isn't quite as it was when it left the shop, having been 'distressed a little' by the scenic workshop to add that touch of realism. "But they tell me it will clean up without too much trouble."

Of course if the event were large, prestigious and long running, then it's likely that the things that I've described will have a budget and be purchased, but their procurement will all probably end up under the remit of stage management or maybe a dedicated props person when it gets to the performance.

3 CUEING OR 'CALLING' THE SHOW: THE PROMPT BOOK

Coming from the backstage technical side of things, for me the biggest and most important element of stage management works are their actions within the performance itself, where they are the catalyst, the instigator, even the conductor of all the technical departments and their efforts to produce a seamless, smooth running performance. Within *Basics – A Beginner's Guide to Stage Lighting* I included a small section covering the actions of stage management and with just a few expansions of the details, make no apology for its inclusion here again. Please also bear in mind that while the following section is rather biased to the lighting within a production, there are many other technical disciplines that require the same format of cueing.

At the lighting technical or plotting session with the lighting designer, control operator and the director sitting at the production desk within the auditorium, there is normally one other person involved – usually the deputy stage manager – the person who is going to 'call' or cue the whole show. While the others are busy getting the lighting states sorted out, the deputy stage manager will be getting down the relevant information into the prompt book so that each lighting change can be given as a cue to the control operator.

Two important points to note: I know that many amateur companies and lots of others who simply don't know any better, will say that "our lighting people take all their cues themselves from reading their own copy of the script." Well not in my world they don't, it's just not possible to read text, watch the stage and work the control desk all at the same time with any degree success, even in a slow moving two-handed play, let alone a fast moving musical. No it all comes down to the DSM, for it's this person's job to bring together all the technical departments so that they are given all the information they need to do the technical job at the right time.

The second critical point which also involves the DSM, is the language used. No, not the profanities, but the actual words and their order when used in talking to the technical departments. Most technical theatre uses a communications system in performance where each operator and the stage manager wears a headset (earphones) with a microphone, so that everybody can give and receive information. Those using such a system for the first time should be (must be) discouraged from idle chatter. The 'comms' network is not in place to discuss the football results, organise the after show party, or any other topic other than the technical job in hand – and at this point what is vitally important is the order of words and the language used.

DSM: "Standby Electrics (LX) cue 47."

Lighting Control: "LX cue 47 standing by."

The stage manager will have agreed the length of the standby period beforehand with all technical department and operators.

DSM: "LX cue 47 GO."

Lighting control will action the cue on the command word GO.

It all looks and sounds very simple and it is, but just put yourself in the position of the DSM who has to give technical cues to all departments: lighting, sound, offstage effects, flies, followspots and any number of others, as well as calling the acting company from the dressing rooms, keeping times of the performance, following the script or score, and don't forget prompting the acting company if needed. If you have a good DSM do all you can to keep him or her, for this person will help make your show a success. A bad one however, who panics at the slightest hint of a problem, can ruin your technical efforts and should be encouraged to find an alternative way of spending their evening.

The point about the language and order of words is that the command word "GO" must be the last word given, so that the control operator, already on standby, is given all of the information again just prior to the command ("Go") to action the cue.

"LX" lets the operator know this is for them and no other technical department; "cue 47" again gives the precise nature of the cue to be performed and "GO" is the exact moment that the change is made or started.

Don't forget that the technical department put on standby should acknowledge this to the stage manager: "LX cue 47 standing by".

I made the comment that the DSM will have agreed the length of the standby period with all of the technical operators beforehand. Getting this small and seemingly insignificant little detail right is in fact very important. Too long spent with the technical operator waiting on standby will cause them to get bored with the waiting and not be attentive when the time comes to action the cue; too short a standby period and the technicians won't have had a chance to gather their thoughts about what action they are about to undertake. Very often the nature and pace of the performance will also affect the standby time. In a slowly paced wordy dramatic piece, a page of text might take a couple of minutes to get through, but in a fast moving musical comedy a page may only last for 30 seconds, so experience on the part of the stage manager will usually help. A standby time of something just less than 30 seconds is what most people feel comfortable with.

But why is this business of the standby, the actual cue and the order of words used so relevant? Because the system of cueing must be geared to the most needful situation, such as when a lighting cue with instant effect must be performed at a precise moment in the action, as when an actor switches on a table lamp or light switch. Yes I know that in the main this type of cue is taken as a visual cue by the lighting operator, but there will come a time when the operator must rely on the DSM to give the cue in exactly the right place, so the method of giving the cue must be correct and the same every time.

So while the lighting designer and operator are getting down the information which is the lighting state, your DSM and the director will be agreeing and noting down exactly where the cue is given in the action or text.

The lighting plotting session will also need at least one other person present, usually a member of the stage management team, who having been involved with the rehearsals will know some of the blocking that has been made and will 'walk' the stage so that when the lighting states have been created, the lighting designer and operator can see and check that all the relevant stage areas are covered.

Remember all of those other technical disciplines; it's not just the lighting which require the notation of cue actions. Others may include sound, followspots, flying, offstage effects, etc and they may not all come together until a first technical or first rehearsal takes place.

In order to achieve all of the cueing that's involved, the stage manager will use a 'prompt book' or 'prompt script' which is laid out in a very specific and ordered style. Most stage management practitioners will have their own individual variations, but in the main they will be based around an individual page of text or libretto, faced by a plain sheet, with two columns (see illustration).

With one page containing the dialogue, or the libretto in the case of a music score, a mark will be made at a specific point of the text or action, and a line will be drawn horizontally across to the lined sheet on the other, where it will

Blocking notes

S/B SOUND Q 12
S/B LX Q 45

① D + S enter thro door
   D x to sofa sits
② S sits on chair
③ D stands to shout
④ D sits
⑤ S x to sofa sits.

SOUND Q 12 } GO
LX Q 45 }

THIS IS YOUR CALL
MISS JONES
MR WILLIAMS

Script

① David: And so I was walking through the park when this boy leapt out at me and shouted "Arh" in a really loud voice!

Sasha: I bet that frightened you

David: Frightened, no. Angry, yes

Sasha: So what did you do next? You didn't run after him did you?
② You know how the doctor said you must be more careful not to strain yourself

David: I didn't run after him as such.....

Sasha: What does that mean? That you walked quickly?!

David: Well I did sort of walk quickly. I followed him down the road and into the park and all the time I was shouting "Come back here, you rude boy" and he kept looking over his shoulder.

Sasha: ③ You must be more careful. He could have come at you with a knife!

David: But it was ten o'clock in the morning and there were lots of people about. Anyway the really interesting thing was that he did actually look a bit frightened. I thought he might shout back at me but he didn't. He just kept moving along, looking over his shoulder.

Sasha: ④ So what happened then?

David: ⑤ Well I could see he was still looking so I took out my mobile as if I was going to call the police but then I thought that a better thing to do was to take his photo!

Sasha: And did you?

David: Did I what?

Example of a professional prompt copy showing blocking and cueing.

end at the column closest to the text. The cue action (either Standby or Go) is then written into the column. The text and lines inserted in this way are often made in pencil, so that changes can easily be made.

This provides a neat and ordered assembly of actions and commands, which the stage management personnel can follow and action as the performance goes along. Of course this all looks quite simple and straightforward, but in real life it's far from that. There will be occasions where cues will be happening in multiples: lighting, sound, flies, offstage effects, etc all happening at once, and there will be many occasions where the standby for one technical discipline may overlap the cue command of another, different discipline. There will be cues that although written as a command, will actually be a visual cue taken by the technical operator. There may be 'follow on' cues, which in fact are not given as cues at all but simply actions made by the technical operator following the completion of the previous cue. There may be calls to be made to the dressing rooms, even where the performance space has the benefit of a live show relay system. Then there is the small matter of the acting company skipping lines of text or action, or even worse mixing up the order in which they deliver them. That can be a real nightmare where the section that they missed out or jumbled up contains cues that are specific or even critical to the production.

One other small function that falls to stage management, specifically the person calling the show, is to keep accurate times of the performance: its start time and duration of each act, and also to fill in a show report. The timings are important for a number of reasons, for when a production has been running for a few days, it will usually settle down into a fairly similar time pattern, probably being just a little shorter than the opening night, as it will 'tighten up' as the acting company get more used to it. Of course this is extremely variable depending upon the style of the piece in performance. Where a wordy drama will normally stay very much the same, a comedy or musical event that may contain some audience reaction, could well vary much more. This type of variation is usually noted within the show report, with comments like "very lively audience tonight, act 2 almost three minutes longer than normal."

Most directors or company managers, indeed theatre managers, will be keeping a watchful eye on the running times of performances. If they start to extend then it may be that the acting company are slowing it down, therefore it will not be running at the pace that the director was happy with, or worse, they may be extending the dialogue with additional words or actions. Of course the piece may be running faster, in which case there may be chunks of text or business missed out. Either way the timings and the show reports from the stage management will keep track of it.

Another important part of the stage management job, but one which we all hope never to call upon is contingency planning. In stage management terms it's a plan of action that is aimed at the continuous and seamless presentation of the performance and of course there are endless ways in which a performance can be affected, from the sudden illness of one of the acting company, to mechanical defects in the set or other technical equipment.

Many of these things may not be able to be controlled by stage management in which case they will just be dealing with the consequences of the event, and their contingency is knowing how best to deal with the crisis unfolding before their eyes – and believe me, the word crisis is not overplayed.

Some of the things I have seen happening during a live performance, let alone the rehearsals, would be unbelievable if scripted into the actual piece of theatre, such as the star of the show (British stage screen and TV actress) who, refusing to give in to a severe stomach upset, insisted on performing, thus requiring stage management to be ready with a strategically placed bucket offstage which she used when being quite violently sick every time she came offstage. Or the occasion where one of the principal singers in a touring grand opera production fell from a balcony on set, breaking her arm in the process, but with only a short break in proceedings to scoop the unfortunate lady out of the footlights, she and the production completed the last 10 minutes of the opera to be greeted with warmer than usual applause at the final curtain. It's these sort of things, not always involving the acting personnel, that stage management contingency planning has to know how to cope with, and don't forget that while these unusual things are going on, stage management still have to run the show and cue all of the other things as if it were a normal performance.

Did I mention the often joked about "never work with children or animals" syndrome? No I think not, but contingency planning is probably the best place to make a note of it. I think it's perhaps the bright lights or an over-warm atmosphere but there's a better than average chance that the animals will make their mark by peeing when they should just be there for set dressing, and if they are rather young and immature I wouldn't leave the children out of this either! Best to keep that mop and bucket handy.

The final, and perhaps the most important part of the contingency plan, is to ensure that the prompt book is clearly marked up as previously described in the format and style that all of the stage management team are familiar with, just in case the team member normally cueing the show is off for some reason, then the person taking over will have a good chance of getting it right.

One personal observation about the stage management personnel who are tasked to call the show is that some are better than others and in my experience, women are far better at it than men. Please don't label this as a sexist observation aimed at confining women to a low-tech menial role, far from it. In fact view it as the reverse and a very big compliment. I'm not about to delve into the psyche of the male versus the female mind, but what I know is that in the main, women don't panic as readily in the highly stressful environment of running a show.

Maybe as others have said in different disciplines over the years, they are simply better at simultaneous multi-tasking, which is exactly what happens

Cueing the show.

in calling a show. Then of course there's the calming influence of having a soft and soothing voice giving you commands when as one of the technical operators, you probably have enough worries of your own to contend with. I'm not saying that men can't do the job, I'm simply making the point that I believe women do it better.

4 THE HARDWARE

It's something of a tradition (but also a practical function) that in the performance activities of stage management you will be expected to wear black clothes. It may be that you will not be required to go onstage during a scene change to set or strike props for the next scene, but just like the order of words involved in cueing, if the format is in place and it's the same every time, you are prepared for anything. So black clothes are the order of the performance day.

I said somewhere at the beginning that there was very little hardware or equipment involved in the tasks of stage management – well by comparison with all the other technical disciplines that's true. But there is one thing which is equipment-based which is worthy of note: the 'prompt corner desk'.

You can see how it is in the terminology used in theatrical performance. I keep playing down the business of the prompt but keep referring to things relating to the word: prompt book, prompt script, prompt corner desk – and you will probably know that in a traditional end-stage space the stage is still talked about

1988 stage manager's desk with peripheral equipment at Sola Kulture House in Norway, photo: John Offord (Lighting+Sound International).

as having a Prompt Side (PS) and an Opposite Prompt Side (OP). You just can't get away from the term even if the action of the prompt is now rarely used.

Incidentally, although the majority of end-stages probably have the stage left side designated as the prompt side, being the location of the prompt desk, it's not unusual to find some places operating with the prompt desk on stage right, affectionately known as 'bastard prompt'. More correctly, the whole area at the downstage left or right position, is normally referred to as the 'prompt corner'.

Going back a little, in the general history and design of the proscenium arch theatre, the prompt corner, sometimes also referred to as the 'working' side of the stage, was the location of almost all of the switching and mechanisms involved in performance use. Things have evolved somewhat in that as many operations are now being controlled electronically, they have been condensed into a smaller and mobile format. Therefore, what was the mass of fixtures and wiring in the prompt corner has now become the more flexible prompt desk that can move around a little, albeit still tied to the original prompt corner position by an umbilical cable.

I am reminded that being Basics, I need to clarify the term Stage Left and Right, since this is something that can cause confusion and is probably the very first thing that stage management learn on day one. Stage Left is 'actor's left' i.e. when standing on a traditional proscenium arch stage looking into the auditorium, your left is stage left. Some people become confused because when looking at the stage from the auditorium, they forget and revert to the normal left and right direction, which of course is incorrect. And while we are dealing with stage direction terms 'Upstage' and 'Downstage', downstage is nearest to the seated audience.

A touring SM desk.

The hardware I referred to as the 'prompt desk' is also quite often referred to as the 'SM (stage management) desk'. As I said, it's now a moveable item. It's a strange mixture: it's part desk, part technical workstation, it's usually quite tall – not a desk that you sit down at – rather something that will cause you to use a high chair or stool. There really isn't such a thing as a regulation prompt/SM desk – they all tend to get populated with equipment to suit the requirements of the venue they are working in. Some will have just the bare essentials: a desktop surface big enough to contain an A4 loose leaf folder, with a light and a means of communication (headset and microphone) linking to all the technical departments, while others will resemble the flight deck of a space shuttle with CCTV monitors, cue lights, telephone ring tone generators, clock, event timers, backstage calls microphone or integral pyrotechnic detonators. The list is almost endless. These things are almost always bespoke and as such the costs associated with them can run into thousands of pounds, but they are the workplace of stage management personnel when it comes to the performance (see illustrations).

There are probably two items of equipment that are a regular part of most prompt desks: the communications system or at least a headset link into it, and the cue light system. Cue lights have been around forever, well almost, certainly since we have been using electricity. The function of a cue light is to give a command (go) to the recipient. It is simply a red (for standby) and green (for go) switch with lights associated to it at the prompt desk. This is wired to a cue light outstation where just the lights are present. These are normally produced

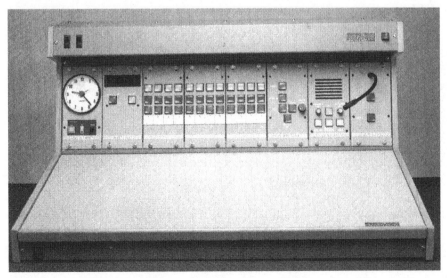

1990 stage manager's desk from Richmond Theatre based on a modular panel construction allowing users to select from a range of control options, photo: Nick Mobsby.

in multiples, so the prompt desk may have 6-10 or more cue light controls all appearing at different places around the stage and technical areas.

Quite a high proportion of new venues will forgo the cue light system altogether, since the advent of the technical communications system means that rather than working on a system of red and green lights, most technical operators will now be in voice link with the stage management personnel running the show. This is much preferred since when working on cue lights only, the operators must assume that their cues are happening in sequence and in a fast moving show with lots of cues, things can rapidly get out of step and out of control. That's not to condemn the cue light system completely. There will be occasions where a light is all that's needed, for instance where an actor is waiting to make an entrance at a critical time relevant to the actions on stage and where they can not wear a communications headset, and it's never a bad idea to have cue lights as a standby or backup to the communications system. The modern cue light system will have one small technical addition to enhance its usability, the cue light outstation will have an 'acknowledge' function, a small button usually between the red and green lights. When this is pushed it makes the red light at the prompt desk stop flashing, so that stage management get an acknowledgement that the person at the cue light outstation is standing by.

Previously I made mention of the timing (running times) of the show and within the description of the prompt desk I listed a clock and an event timer. It's precisely these timing requirements that will use the event timer, but of course the stage management person running the show could simply note down the times. However, it's far easier if their workplace contains this function.

As the workplace from which to control all of the technical things involved, the prompt desk will usually have a line of sight view of the performance stage, even if only from the side. However, due to the nature and shape of the set and scenery, this is not always the case, which can cause problems. Enter another wonder of the modern age: the CCTV camera and monitor. In its ultimate form, this not only provides a full colour image of the stage viewed from the auditorium, but with infrared imaging can provide useful information even in blackout conditions. One or more small monitor screens are normally built into the prompt desk providing the stage manager with a clear view of the stage.

I have made many references to technical communications or 'comms' or 'intercom' for short, so some more detailed information is needed, in part taken from *Basics – A Beginner's Guide to Stage Sound.*

The first thing to understand is that the technical communications equipment involved is totally separate from any performance related equipment. The hub of the technical communications system is called a 'master' or 'base' station. This is simply a small dedicated amplifier that will run either two or three 'rings' or separate circuits. Each ring or circuit is wired to outlet terminations in various places, usually identified as 'A' and 'B' ring, the users connecting to whichever one is designated for their use.

The stage management person who is cueing the show will often be working in close proximity to the base station, which may be built into the prompt desk. However, sometimes the base station is at another location, with only a connection point at the prompt desk. Whatever the location, stage management will choose and select which of the rings are going to receive the cues given. It may be that lighting and sound are set up on ring A, while everyone else is on ring B. There is no particular right and wrong way to do this, it is a matter of personal preference on the part of the stage management and technical teams involved, and may to some degree be dictated by the layout of the building and it can change from production to production, as needs arise.

The users of this type of system will each wear a headset, either single or double muff (earpiece) type, which has a small boom microphone attached. This headset connects into a small belt pack which, as the name implies, clips onto the user's belt. A relatively short flexible cable 3 to 5 metres long then connects the belt pack to the nearest A or B ring connection point. The belt pack will have an on/off control switch for the microphone, a volume control for the headset, and a 'call' light and switch, which simply flashes all the other call lights in all the other belt packs connected to the ring. This relatively simple set-up permits the spoken word flow of information between stage management and all the technical operators and is regarded as an industry standard requirement for all performance arts venues (see illustrations overleaf).

You are probably thinking, fine, I accept the need for the technical communications link in getting the cueing information to the technical operators, but why can't it use radio signals, like radio microphones? Well, if you have the budget you can do, but remember unlike a radio microphone, this function needs to send and receive, so the costs are double. Anyway, for most technical operators, their workstation is a fixed location: lighting control desk, sound mixer, followspot, etc so the mobility of a radio signal system is not that vital. In fact it's not until you get to the larger venues that you will

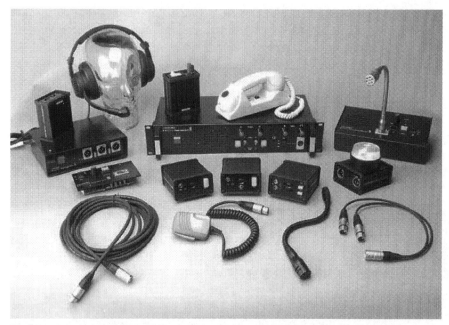

TechPro Intercom communications equipment showing headset, handset, base stations, belt packs and accessories, courtesy Canford Audio.

find one or two wireless (UHF send and receive) systems are used, connecting to the fixed wiring set-up to provide the flexibility needed by people who need to be mobile but still need to be on the technical communications system.

There are quite a few variations within the technical communications equipment. There are dual circuit belt packs, so that the wearer can pick up both the A and B ring information, there are loudspeaker outstations for greenrooms and other non-stage areas and telephone handsets, which may be used by the FOH staff to give clearance to stage management as previously mentioned. The planning of the technical communications system can be quite a complex matter, however in its simplest form, it can be provided as a temporary system, as long as you can cope with the loose cable all over the place. Just to keep things sensible, the wiring used, indeed even the short link cables, are the same specification as used for performance sound microphones: a twin screened signal cable being terminated in a 3 pin XLR connector.

So in terms of the hardware involved in the life of stage management, that's about it: the prompt desk and all it contains. Of course, the real trick is knowing how to use it, which all comes down to the skill and expertise of the stage management operator. Oh, one last thing on the hardware topic – bring a torch because an awful lot of stage management work during the performance will involve you working in the semi-dark or even blackout light conditions.

5 TRAINING FOR STAGE MANAGEMENT

You have belonged to the stage management department of a local amateur company. You might have stage managed some productions in school and you may have even been on work experience at your local theatre. You are pretty sure that you want a career as a stage manager but how do you go about it?

If you know this at 16, there are two options: A levels or a BTEC in Performing Arts which may contain some technical elements or a BTEC in Production which normally concentrates more on the backstage role. After this the option for many people is a course at a drama school or a higher education establishment. There is invaluable information on the National Council for Drama Training website (www.ncdt.co.uk) and also on the Council of Drama Schools website (www.drama.ac.uk). These two websites point you towards what type of courses are available, where they are, how long they are and how much they cost. Each individual school will give you more information about their courses and about what kind of career you can expect upon graduation. If you can, go and visit each potential school which will then give you a much clearer idea of where you want to go and study.

If going to drama school is not an option for you, there could be another way using the Creative and Cultural Skills Organisation (www.ccskills.org. uk) who are setting up Creative Apprenticeships in order to provide training and education for all. This is still in the early stages of its development but could see the return of a more "learning on the job" type system.

Before this becomes reality, your best option is to start working at your nearest theatre in any capacity backstage that you can. This may initially be as get-in or get-out crew, or followspot operator, or dresser. Once you have worked or are working there, you will get a much clearer idea of what kind of backstage work you will want to do and indeed if stage management is what you want.

Try to talk to the local stage management, arrange your own work placement, ask to be allowed to observe – most people don't object if it can be arranged with the management and provided it means they get an extra pair of hands in a busy rehearsal period! There is no substitute for seeing how it's done professionally, and sooner or later this will pay off in terms of a job – but this route may take you a little longer before you get to the job you really want than if you were able to go to drama school.

CCSkills are also creating National Occupational Standards for all backstage professions; and looking to introduce work-based qualifications to achieve them. In other words, you could have your work experience and on-the-job training validated by being assessed in the work place in the future.

Once you are in your chosen training field it can be time to consider joining the entertainment union, Equity (www.equity.org.uk) and/or the professional association for stage managers, the SMA (www.stagemanagementassociation. co.uk). Both bodies have student membership that can help to keep you up to date with current practice and allow you to meet other members. If you are working with an amateur group, you can still join the SMA as an associate member and benefit from their publications, website, information services and meetings.

Finally – a word for the more mature potential stage manager. There are a number of people each year who decide that they would still like to work in professional stage management and there are a few courses available at post-graduate level. These can be found via the NCDT and the CDS websites and just because they are called post-graduate it may not mean that you have to have a degree. More likely entry will be based on relevant experience.

So whatever your age: if you want to be a stage manager, go find out how!

6 CONCLUSIONS

Something that's perhaps a little strange and probably the main difference between professional stage management and that within an amateur or education base, is that it's quite likely that within the professional ranks, the team of stage management will be itinerant jobbing stage management people, moving from job to job and thus setting up home, even on a short term and temporary basis. Yes, of course there are many towns and cities across the country where theatre companies employ resident stage management personnel, but even these venues will take on new members of the team for short-term contracts depending upon the nature of the productions involved, and of course in the summer months there are those events and seasonal activities which only exist for a few months, not forgetting the great British tradition of pantomime which brings about the same sort of thing in the winter.

I hope that for those of you entering the world of theatre and the performing arts, this basics publication has provided at least in insight into what stage management is all about and why it's vitally important in the process of mounting a successful production. As you come to the end of your formal stage management training, probably from a drama school, you will be both excited and uncertain about what waits for you in your first taste of professional theatre work. Excited that at last you will be getting into the real world of the performing arts, uncertain because although your first steps may be as a lowly ASM you know that you will one day be the stage manager on a West End musical. Some of you may have the rather traditional misconception that it's a glamorous job, being involved with the 'stars' of a performing company. Some will take the stage management route but as an end to another facet of the entertainment industry, such as arts management. In fact years ago, being an ASM was seen as a way to becoming an actor, but these days it is rarely so. The one fact that is common to all who embark in a profession allied to the performing arts, is that given the numbers that set out on this career path every year, only a very small percentage actually see it through into a long term way of life and that includes those who intended to stay within stage management. You will all have heard the comments before: poor rates of pay, long hours, seemingly thankless tasks, certainly very little glamour and usually very little appreciation. So why do people put themselves through it all? Well one reason may be that when you have mastered the craft, indeed some might even describe it as an 'art form', you will get an enormous level of self satisfaction in doing the job and getting it right.

I'll close with perhaps one of my first, and lasting, recollections of the 'unflappable' stage manager, which even now, many years later, really says it all about the job. In the early to mid 1960s, the Saddler's Wells Opera Company as it was then, toured a landmark production of Wagner's The Flying Dutchman, the staging of which is difficult enough to achieve within a large opera house and on tour even more challenging. One of the main technical headaches was the appearance of the Dutchman's ship out of the mist, an effect created by projected images and lighting (designed by Charles Bristow) which in its day was real ground-breaking stuff. This called for rather a lot of lighting cues all coming close together at the end of the first act.

In today's technological age this sort of thing isn't much of a problem as lighting changes can be made at the touch of a button, but back then when everything was mechanical, not even electronic, it was a bit of a trial. So with lots of temporary wire-wound resistance dimmers set up on side of stage right next to the prompt corner and with all cues being given by cue lights, I can still remember the stage manager turning to me and asking, "What cue have you just done?" to which I replied: "cue 28". It was probably quite obvious to the stage manager that things didn't look quite as they should, but without any panic or change in the voice he simply said, "Well we've just done cue 32 so catch up as quick as you can!"

STAGE MANAGEMENT ASSOCIATION
55 Farringdon Rd, London EC1M 3JB
Tel: 020-7242 9250
website: www.stagemanagementassociation.co.uk

The Stage Management Association (SMA) is the professional body supporting and representing Stage Management in the UK.

Amongst the services it provides are:

- representation of members and the profession within the industry
- promotion of stage management in the media
- practical advice on a range of issues from contracts to props to digs
- bi-monthly magazine Cueline with news, views and in-depth analysis
- website – soon to be relaunched with a much bigger members' only area
- career development and training
- meetings, talks, tours, forums
- publications and information
- network of stage managers to draw on
- help finding work through Free List, listing on Spotlight Interactive and an in-house jobs list

For further information and details of how to join, contact the Administrator, Stage Management Association, 55 Farringdon Road, London, EC1M 3JB, Tel.020 7242 9250   Fax 020 7242 9303

website: www.stagemanagementassociation.co.uk
e-mail: admin@stagemanagementassociation.co.uk

A Company Limited by Guarantee (England and Wales) Registration No. 3819176.

FURTHER READING

Stage Management – A Career Guide available through the SMA website
www.stagemanagementassociation.co.uk

Stage Management – The Essential Handbook by Gail Pallin
Nick Hern Books ISBN: 978 1854597342

Essential Guide to Stage Management, Lighting and Sound
(Essential Guides to the Performing Arts) by Scott Palmer
Hodder Arnold ISBN: 978 0340721138

Stage Management: A Practical Guide by Soozie Copley and
Philippa Kilner
The Crowood Press ISBN: 978 1861264534

Production Management: Making Shows Happen – A Practical Guide
by Peter Dean
The Crowood Press ISBN: 978 1861264510

Essentials of Stage Management by Peter Maccoy
A & C Black ISBN: 978 0713665284

Stage Management and Theatre Administration by Terry Hawkins and
Pauline Menear
Phaidon Press Ltd ISBN: 978 0714825168

Stage Management – a gentle art by Daniel Bond
Routledge ISBN: 978 0878300679

GLOSSARY

This list is by no means comprehensive. It is only intended as a quick reference to those names and phrases which cause most confusion to the beginner.

ASM   Assistant Stage Manager.

Blocking   The instructions by the director or choreographer in positioning the acting company in a particular position on stage, being noted down by stage management.

Calls   The ½ hour, ¼ hour, 5 minutes, Act One beginners: 'calls' made by stage management to the acting company.

CCTV   Closed Circuit Television.

Contingency Planning
Plans for actions required to cope or cover for accidents or technical shortcomings within a performance.

Cue   The action by stage management (often as a spoken command word "Go") to any technical operator.

Cue Lights System of small red and green lights, operated by stage management, giving 'standby' and 'go' commands at various places around the stage area and technical areas.

DSM   Deputy Stage Manager.

Drying   A member of the acting company forgetting their lines, causing stage management to provide a prompt.

Dressing Room Show Relay
The amplified sound from the stage, fed into each dressing room, also including "calls" from stage management to the acting company.

Equity   The actor's trade union.

FOH (Front of House)
The public areas of a theatre or performance space.

Marking or Setting out
The stage management function of marking out the rehearsal space floor with a representation of the set and stage area.

Prompt Words spoken sotto voce by stage management (or a dedicated prompter) in order to re-start the member of the acting company who has forgotten their lines.

Prompt Book / Script / Libretto
A book containing the sung or spoken words of the show laid out in a specific style, which will also contain notations of the cues given to technical departments.

Prompt Desk / Prompt Corner
The workplace within the performance space, from which the stage manager controls all the technical departments. As a technical feature the prompt desk will contain switching and control for all systems and equipment used during performance activities.

Props (Properties)
Any item or article found on stage not specifically a part of the set or scenery.

Read Through
Usually the first meeting of the acting company when they will sit together reading through the text of the work to be performed.

Show Report
A brief written report made by stage management about each performance, its start and finish times and any noteworthy events.

Stage Left and Right
In a traditional proscenium arch or end stage pertaining to the actors left when standing on stage, thus stage right being opposite. This orientation is then retained, all references to stage left/right being the same, from whatever viewing point.

Standby The warning (standby) given by stage management, prior to a cue being given.

Technical Communications
Almost all performance spaces will need a means whereby the operators of the various elements of technical equipment can communicate with each

other and receive instructions during the performance.

Walking the stage

The action (normally by a member of stage management) in walking and standing in each part of the stage used in performance, normally to check the lighting coverage during the technical plotting session.

Titles Published by Entertainment Technology Press

ABC of Theatre Jargon *Francis Reid* **£9.95** ISBN 1904031099
This glossary of theatrical terminology explains the common words and phrases that are used in normal conversation between actors, directors, designers, technicians and managers.

Aluminium Structures in the Entertainment Industry *Peter Hind* **£24.95**
ISBN 1904031064
Aluminium Structures in the Entertainment Industry aims to educate the reader in all aspects of the design and safe usage of temporary and permanent aluminium structures specific to the entertainment industry – such as roof structures, PA towers, temporary staging, etc.

Autocad – A Handbook for Theatre Users *David Ripley* **£24.95** ISBN 1904031315
From 'Setting Up' to 'Drawing in Three Dimensions' via 'Drawings Within Drawings', this compact and fully illustrated guide to AutoCAD covers everything from the basics to full colour rendering and remote plotting.

Basics – A Beginner's Guide to Lighting Design *Peter Coleman* **£9.95** ISBN 1904031412
The fourth in the author's 'Basics' series, this title covers the subject area in four main sections: The Concept, Practical Matters, Related Issues and The Design Into Practice. In an area that is difficult to be difinitive, there are several things that cross all the boundaries of all lighting design and it's these areas that the author seeks to help with.

Basics – A Beginner's Guide to Special Effects *Peter Coleman* **£9.95** ISBN 1904031331
This title introduces newcomers to the world of special effects. It describes all types of special effects including pyrotechnic, smoke and lighting effects, projections, noise machines, etc. It places emphasis on the safe storage, handling and use of pyrotechnics.

Basics – A Beginner's Guide to Stage Lighting *Peter Coleman* **£9.95** ISBN 190403120X
This title does what it says: it introduces newcomers to the world of stage lighting. It will not teach the reader the art of lighting design, but will teach beginners much about the 'nuts and bolts' of stage lighting.

Basics: A Beginner's Guide to Stage Management *Peter Coleman* **£7.95**
ISBN 9781904031475
The fifth in Peter Coleman's popular 'Basics' series, this title provides a practical insight into, and the definition of, the role of stage management. Further chapters describe Cueing or 'Calling' the Show (the Prompt Book), and the Hardware and Training for Stage Management. This is a book about people and systems, without which most of the technical equipment used by others in the performance workplace couldn't function.

Basics – A Beginner's Guide to Stage Sound *Peter Coleman* **£9.95** ISBN 1904031277
This title does what it says: it introduces newcomers to the world of stage sound. It will not teach the reader the art of sound design, but will teach beginners much about the background to sound reproduction in a theatrical environment.

Building Better Theaters *Michael Mell* **£16.95** 1904031404
A title within our Consultancy Series, this book describes the process of designing a theater,

from the initial decision to build through to opening night. Michael Mell's book provides a step-by-step guide to the design and construction of performing arts facilities. Chapters discuss: assembling your team, selecting an architect, different construction methods, the architectural design process, construction of the theater, theatrical systems and equipment, the stage, backstage, the auditorium, ADA requirements and the lobby. Each chapter clearly describes what to expect and how to avoid surprises. It is a must-read for architects, planners, performing arts groups, educators and anyone who may be considering building or renovating a theater.

Close Protection – The Softer Skills *Geoffrey Padgham* **£11.95** ISBN 1904031390
This is the first educational book in a new 'Security Series' for Entertainment Technology Press, and it coincides with the launch of the new 'Protective Security Management' Foundation Degree at Buckinghamshire Chilterns University College (BCUC). The author is a former full-career Metropolitan Police Inspector from New Scotland Yard with 27 years' experience of close protection (CP). For 22 of those years he specialised in operations and senior management duties with the Royalty Protection Department at Buckingham Palace, followed by five years in the private security industry specialising in CP training design and delivery. His wealth of protection experience comes across throughout the text, which incorporates sound advice and exceptional practical guidance, subtly separating fact from fiction. This publication is an excellent form of reference material for experienced operatives, students and trainees.

A Comparative Study of Crowd Behaviour at Two Major Music Events
Chris Kemp, Iain Hill, Mick Upton **£7.95** ISBN 1904031250
A compilation of the findings of reports made at two major live music concerts, and in particular crowd behaviour, which is followed from ingress to egress.

Copenhagen Opera House *Richard Brett and John Offord* **£32.00** ISBN 1904031420
Completed in a little over three years, the Copenhagen Opera House opened with a royal gala performance on 15th January 2005. Built on a spacious brown-field site, the building is a landmark venue and this book provides the complete technical background story to an opera house set to become a benchmark for future design and planning. Sixteen chapters by relevant experts involved with the project cover everything from the planning of the auditorium and studio stage, the stage engineering, stage lighting and control and architectural lighting through to acoustic design and sound technology plus technical summaries.

Electrical Safety for Live Events *Marco van Beek* **£16.95** ISBN 1904031285
This title covers electrical safety regulations and good pracitise pertinent to the entertainment industries and includes some basic electrical theory as well as clarifying the "do's and don't's" of working with electricity.

The Exeter Theatre Fire *David Anderson* **£24.95** ISBN 1904031137
This title is a fascinating insight into the events that led up to the disaster at the Theatre Royal, Exeter, on the night of September 5th 1887. The book details what went wrong, and the lessons that were learned from the event.

Fading Light – A Year in Retirement *Francis Reid* **£14.95** ISBN 1904031358
Francis Reid, the lighting industry's favourite author, describes a full year in retirement. "Old age is much more fun than I expected," he says. Fading Light describes visits and

experiences to the author's favourite theatres and opera houses, places of relaxation and re-visits to scholarly intitutions.

Focus on Lighting Technology *Richard Cadena* **£17.95** ISBN 1904031145
This concise work unravels the mechanics behind modern performance lighting and appeals to designers and technicians alike. Packed with clear, easy-to-read diagrams, the book provides excellent explanations behind the technology of performance lighting.

Health and Safety Aspects in the Live Music Industry *Chris Kemp, Iain Hill* **£30.00** ISBN 1904031226
This title includes chapters on various safety aspects of live event production and is written by specialists in their particular areas of expertise.

Health and Safety Management in the Live Music and Events Industry *Chris Hannam* **£25.95** ISBN 1904031307
This title covers the health and safety regulations and their application regarding all aspects of staging live entertainment events, and is an invaluable manual for production managers and event organisers.

Hearing the Light – 50 Years Backstage *Francis Reid* **£24.95** ISBN 1904031188
This highly enjoyable memoir delves deeply into the theatricality of the industry. The author's almost fanatical interest in opera, his formative period as lighting designer at Glyndebourne and his experiences as a theatre administrator, writer and teacher make for a broad and unique background.

An Introduction to Rigging in the Entertainment Industry *Chris Higgs* **£24.95** ISBN 1904031129
This book is a practical guide to rigging techniques and practices and also thoroughly covers safety issues and discusses the implications of working within recommended guidelines and regulations.

Let There be Light – Entertainment Lighting Software Pioneers in Interview
Robert Bell **£32.00** ISBN 1904031242
Robert Bell interviews a distinguished group of software engineers working on entertainment lighting ideas and products.

Lighting for Roméo and Juliette *John Offord* **£26.95** ISBN 1904031161
John Offord describes the making of the Vienna State Opera production from the lighting designer's viewpoint – from the point where director Jürgen Flimm made his decision not to use scenery or sets and simply employ the expertise of LD Patrick Woodroffe.

Lighting Systems for TV Studios *Nick Mobsby* **£45.00** ISBN 1904031005
Lighting Systems for TV Studios, now in its second edition, is the first book specifically written on the subject and has become the 'standard' resource work for studio planning and design covering the key elements of system design, luminaires, dimming, control, data networks and suspension systems as well as detailing the infrastructure items such as cyclorama, electrical and ventilation. Sensibly TV lighting principles are explained and some history on TV broadcasting, camera technology and the equipment is provided to help set the scene! The second edition includes applications for sine wave and distributed dimming, moving lights, Ethernet and new cool lamp technology.

Lighting Techniques for Theatre-in-the-Round *Jackie Staines* **£24.95**
ISBN 1904031013
Lighting Techniques for Theatre-in-the-Round is a unique reference source for those working on lighting design for theatre-in-the-round for the first time. It is the first title to be published specifically on the subject, it also provides some anecdotes and ideas for more challenging shows, and attempts to blow away some of the myths surrounding lighting in this format.

Lighting the Stage *Francis Reid* **£14.95** ISBN 1904031080
Lighting the Stage discusses the human relationships involved in lighting design – both between people, and between these people and technology. The book is written from a highly personal viewpoint and its 'thinking aloud' approach is one that Francis Reid has used in his writings over the past 30 years.

Model National Standard Conditions *ABTT/DSA/LGLA* **£20.00** ISBN 1904031110
These *Model National Standard Conditions* covers operational matters and complement *The Technical Standards for Places of Entertainment*, which describes the physical requirements for building and maintaining entertainment premises.

Mr Phipps' Theatre *Mark Jones, John Pick* **£17.95** ISBN: 1904031382
Mark Jones and John Pick describe "The Sensational Story of Eastbourne's Royal Hippodrome" – formerly Eastbourne Theatre Royal. An intriguing narrative, the book sets the story against a unique social history of the town. Peter Longman, former director of The Theatres Trust, provides the Foreword.

Pages From Stages *Anthony Field* **£17.95** ISBN 1904031269
Anthony Field explores the changing style of theatres including interior design, exterior design, ticket and seat prices, and levels of service, while questioning whether the theatre still exists as a place of entertainment for regular theatre-goers.

Performing Arts Technical Training Handbook 2007/2008 *ed: John Offord* **£19.95** ISBN 9781904031451
Published in association with the ABTT (Association of British Theatre Technicians), this important Handbook includes fully detailed and indexed entries describing courses on backstage crafts offered by over 100 universities and colleges across the UK. A completely new research project, with accompanying website, the title also includes articles with advice for those considering a career 'behind the scenes', together with contact information and descriptions of the major organisations involved with industry training – plus details of companies offering training within their own premises. The Handbook will be kept in print, with a major revision annually.

Practical Dimming *Nick Mobsby* **£22.95** ISBN 19040313447
This important and easy to read title covers the history of electrical and electronic dimming, how dimmers work, current dimmer types from around the world, planning of a dimming system, looking at new sine wave dimming technology and distributed dimming. Integration of dimming into different performance venues as well as the necessary supporting electrical systems are fully detailed. Significant levels of information are provided on the many different forms and costs of potential solutions as well as how to plan specific solutions. Architectural dimming for the likes of hotels, museums and shopping centres are included. Practical Dimming is a companion book to Practical DMX and is designed for all involved in the use, operation and design of dimming systems.

Practical DMX *Nick Mobsby* **£16.95** ISBN 1904031368
In this highly topical and important title the author details the principles of DMX, how to plan a network, how to choose equipment and cables, with data on products from around the world, and how to install DMX networks for shows and on a permanently installed basis. The easy style of the book and the helpful fault finding tips, together with a review of different DMX testing devices provide an ideal companion for all lighting technicians and system designers. An introduction to Ethernet and Canbus networks are provided as well tips on analogue networks and protocol conversion. This title has been recently updated to include a new chapter on Remote Device Management that became an international standard in Summer 2006.

Practical Guide to Health and Safety in the Entertainment Industry
Marco van Beek **£14.95** ISBN 1904031048
This book is designed to provide a practical approach to Health and Safety within the Live Entertainment and Event industry. It gives industry-pertinent examples, and seeks to break down the myths surrounding Health and Safety.

Production Management *Joe Aveline* **£17.95** ISBN 1904031102
Joe Aveline's book is an in-depth guide to the role of the Production Manager, and includes real-life practical examples and 'Aveline's Fables' – anecdotes of his experiences with real messages behind them.

Rigging for Entertainment: Regulations and Practice *Chris Higgs* **£19.95**
ISBN 1904031218
Continuing where he left off with his highly successful *An Introduction to Rigging in the Entertainment Industry*, Chris Higgs' second title covers the regulations and use of equipment in greater detail.

Rock Solid Ethernet *Wayne Howell* **£24.95** ISBN 1904031293
Although aimed specifically at specifiers, installers and users of entertainment industry systems, this book will give the reader a thorough grounding in all aspects of computer networks, whatever industry they may work in. The inclusion of historical and technical 'sidebars' make for an enjoyable as well as informative read.

Sixty Years of Light Work *Fred Bentham* **£26.95** ISBN 1904031072
This title is an autobiography of one of the great names behind the development of modern stage lighting equipment and techniques.

Sound for the Stage *Patrick Finelli* **£24.95** ISBN 1904031153
Patrick Finelli's thorough manual covering all aspects of live and recorded sound for performance is a complete training course for anyone interested in working in the field of stage sound, and is a must for any student of sound.

Stage Lighting Design in Britain: The Emergence of the Lighting Designer,
1881-1950 *Nigel Morgan* **£17.95** ISBN 190403134X
This book sets out to ascertain the main course of events and the controlling factors that determined the emergence of the theatre lighting designer in Britain, starting with the introduction of incandescent electric light to the stage, and ending at the time of the first public lighting design credits around 1950. The book explores the practitioners, equipment, installations and techniques of lighting design.

Stage Lighting for Theatre Designers *Nigel Morgan* **£17.95** ISBN 1904031196
This is an updated second edition of Nigel Morgan's popular book for students of theatre design – outlining all the techniques of stage lighting design.

Technical Marketing Techniques *David Brooks, Andy Collier, Steve Norman* **£24.95** ISBN 190403103X
Technical Marketing is a novel concept, recently defined and elaborated by the authors of this book, with business-to-business companies competing in fast developing technical product sectors.

Technical Standards for Places of Entertainment *ABTT/DSA* **£30.00** ISBN 1904031056
Technical Standards for Places of Entertainment details the necessary physical standards required for entertainment venues.

Theatre Engineering and Stage Machinery *Toshiro Ogawa* **£30.00** ISBN 9781904031024
Theatre Engineering and Stage Machinery is a unique reference work covering every aspect of theatrical machinery and stage technology in global terms, and across the complete historical spectrum. Revised February 2007.

Theatre Lighting in the Age of Gas *Terence Rees* **£24.95** ISBN 190403117X
Entertainment Technology Press has republished this valuable historic work previously produced by the Society for Theatre Research in 1978. *Theatre Lighting in the Age of Gas* investigates the technological and artistic achievements of theatre lighting engineers from the 1700s to the late Victorian period.

Theatre Space: A Rediscovery Reported *Francis Reid* **£19.95** ISBN 1904031439
In the post-war world of the 1950s and 60s, the format of theatre space became a matter for a debate that aroused passions of an intensity unknown before or since. The proscenium arch was clearly identified as the enemy, accused of forming a barrier to disrupt the relations between the actor and audience. An uneasy fellow-traveller at the time, Francis Reid later recorded his impressions whilst enjoying performances or working in theatres old and new and this book is an important collection of his writings in various theatrical journals from 1969-2001 including his contribution to the Cambridge Guide to the Theatre in 1988. It reports some of the flavour of the period when theatre architecture was rediscovering its past in a search to establish its future.

Theatres of Achievement *John Higgins* **£29.95** ISBN: 1904031374
John Higgins affectionately describes the history of 40 distinguished UK theatres in a personal tribute, each uniquely illustrated by the author. Completing each profile is colour photography by Adrian Eggleston.

Theatric Tourist *Francis Reid* **£19.95** ISBN 9781904031468
Theatric Tourist is the delightful story of Francis Reid's visits across more than 50 years to theatres, theatre museums, performances and even movie theme parks. In his inimitable style, the author involves the reader within a personal experience of venues from the Legacy of Rome to theatres of the Renaissance and Eighteenth Century Baroque and the Gustavian Theatres of Stockholm. His performance experiences include Wagner in Beyreuth, the Pleasures of Tivoli and Wayang in Singapore. This is a 'must have' title for those who are as "incurably stagestruck" as the author.

Walt Disney Concert Hall – The Backstage Story *Patricia MacKay & Richard Pilbrow*
£28.95 ISBN 1904031234
Spanning the 16-year history of the design and construction of the Walt Disney Concert Hall, this book provides a fresh and detailed behind the scenes story of the design and technology from a variety of viewpoints. This is the first book to reveal the "process" of the design of a concert hall.

Yesterday's Lights – A Revolution Reported *Francis Reid* **£26.95** ISBN 1904031323
Set to help new generations to be aware of where the art and science of theatre lighting is coming from – and stimulate a nostalgia trip for those who lived through the period, Francis Reid's latest book has over 350 pages dedicated to the task, covering the 'revolution' from the fifties through to the present day. Although this is a highly personal account of the development of lighting design and technology and he admits that there are 'gaps', you'd be hard put to find anything of significance missing.

Go to www.etbooks.co.uk for full details of above titles and secure online ordering facilities.